KANGAROO

by Caroline Arnold
Photographs by Richard Hewett

WILLIAM MORROW & COMPANY, INC. · New York

PHOTO CREDITS: Permission to use the following photograph is gratefully acknowledged: Zoological Society of San Diego, p. 17.

Library of Congress Cataloging-in-Publication Data: Arnold, Caroline. Kangaroo. Summary: Discusses the kangaroo family, their characteristics and behavior, and, in particular, the experiences of an Australian couple with an orphaned baby kangaroo during his first year in which they prepared him to be on his own. 1. Gray kangaroo—Juvenile literature. 2. Kangaroos—Juvenile literature. 3. Wildlife rescue—Juvenile literature. [1. Kangaroos] I. Hewett, Richard, ill. II. Title. QL737.M35A73   1987   599.2   86-18103   ISBN 0-688-06480-9 | ISBN 0-688-06481-7 (lib. bdg.)

ACKNOWLEDGMENTS

We are grateful to many people for helping us on this project. First, we want to thank Qantas Airways and Terry Bransdon of the Australian Information Service, whose assistance made it possible for us to go to Australia to take the photographs and do research for the book. We thank Irma and Les Melton and Mrs. Lilian Melton for sharing Sport with us. We also thank Pat Robertson and his staff, who welcomed us to the Lone Pine Koala Sanctuary in Brisbane, Australia, and so graciously gave us their time and cooperation. Thanks also to Dwyte Walton and his family for their help with the rufous bettong, Neville and Jane Davis for introducing us to Sport, and John Hughes for his time and advice. Lastly, we want to thank our editor, Andrea Curley, for her enthusiasm and encouragement throughout this project.

*F*rom the back porch of their country house in Wellington Point, Queensland, Irma and Les Melton could see the Pacific Ocean where it met the Australian shore. The trees nearby were noisy with the calls of magpies and parrots, and next to the flowers in the garden below, a young kangaroo contentedly nibbled the green grass.

One night four months earlier, the Meltons had received a telephone call from a friend. "I have found a baby kangaroo," their friend said. "His mother was killed by hunters, and he is too young to care for himself. Can you keep him until he is big enough to be on his own?" The Meltons had never cared for a kangaroo before, but they loved animals and wanted to try to help this orphan.

"Yes," they said. "Bring him over."

When the kangaroo arrived, he looked like a tiny bundle of soft gray fur with spindly legs. The Meltons decided to name him Sport. Then they called the wildlife service to find out the best way to care for him. They learned that they would have to feed him a special formula and were warned not to give him cow's milk because this would make him sick. The Meltons followed these feeding instructions carefully, but even so, it took a week for the young kangaroo to adjust to his new diet. The Meltons were glad when he finally settled down to a regular schedule of four bottles a day.

The wildlife service also issued them a permit to keep the baby kangaroo. It is against the law in Australia to keep any wild animal as a pet. At the end of six months Sport would go to a wildlife preserve.

NATIONAL PARKS
AND WILDLIFE
SERVICE

Authority to keep sick, injured or emaciated fauna

Fauna Conservation Act 1974—1978, Section 24

By virtue of the delegated powers and authorities vested in me under the provisions of the Fauna Conservation Act 1974—1979,

I _Alan Edward Queen NATTRASS_

do hereby authorise _MRS I MELTON_

of _25 Arthur St, Wellington Point 4160._

to hold, keep and care for the fauna listed in the Schedule below

at _above address._

subject to the following terms and conditions:

1. Such fauna in your possession must have been found injured, sick or in an emaciated condition.
2. Such fauna must be liberated back into the wild when it can fend for itself in the wild or otherwise be disposed of as directed by the Conservator of Fauna.
3. Notification to be given to the nearest Queensland National Parks and Wildlife Service Field Officer prior to the release of the fauna or upon its death.
4. The fauna must be kept in accordance with the provisions of the Fauna Conservation Act and Regulations and also the Local Council By-Laws.
5. The fauna must not cause a nuisance to neighbours or other persons.
6. This authority shall remain in force until cancelled by the Conservator of Fauna or until such fauna is liberated into the wild.
7. _This permit expires on 30-2-86._

Schedule

1 Grey (juvenile) Kangaroo.

Dated at _Moggill_

this _30th_ day

of _August_ 19 _85_

Every year many young kangaroos are orphaned. In some cases their mothers are killed by wild dogs, called dingoes, that live in Australia. In other cases the mothers are killed by people, either by hunting or by accident. In areas where kangaroos live near roads, signs warn drivers to be careful. Kangaroos often leap across roads and get hit by cars.

Before 1629, when European explorers first came to Australia, the only people living there were the aborigines. Like the natives, the first Europeans killed a few kangaroos for meat and fur. Later, farmers and ranchers began to settle the land. They cleared forests for fields and dug waterholes for cattle and sheep. Some kinds, or species, of kangaroos that lived in forests began to disappear. Others that lived on open land began to multiply. When kangaroos ate the grass meant for cattle and sheep, the ranchers became angry. They started to kill kangaroos by the thousands.

Today, only limited hunting of kangaroos for fur and meat is allowed. Some people think even stricter laws should be made to protect all kangaroos. They feel that some kinds of kangaroos may become extinct—disappear completely—if too many are killed or if the land they live on is changed too much. Today, scientists are studying kangaroos to find out how many there are, where they live, and what they eat. Only as people learn more about them can a proper balance for land use by people and kangaroos be found.

Red kangaroo

Agile wallaby

Members of the kangaroo family are found only in Australia, New Guinea, Indonesia, and neighboring islands. They are found in almost every kind of landscape, including open plains, dry river bottoms, and forests. Some species of kangaroos even spend most of their lives in trees! Each kind of kangaroo has adapted, or learned to live, in one special environment.

There are fifty-eight different species of kangaroos, and they all belong to one of two large groups. One group is the macropods, which means "big foot." These include all the kangaroos, wallabies, pademelons, quokka, and wallaroos, or euros. All the animals in this group are big, with large hind legs. The biggest of the macropods is the red kangaroo, which can stand seven feet tall and weigh up to two hundred pounds!

The second group, the potoroids, are much smaller than the macropods. They include the rat kangaroos, bettongs, and potoroos. One of the most unusual of the potoroids is the burrowing boodie, the only kangaroo that lives underground. The smallest kangaroo is the musky rat kangaroo, which weighs only one pound! It is also the only kangaroo that produces twins. All others have just one baby at a time.

Rufous bettong

13

Male gray kangaroo

Sport is an eastern gray kangaroo, one of the most commonly seen kangaroos. This type, or the closely related western gray kangaroo, is found throughout Australia. It is the second largest kangaroo in size. A fully grown male gray kangaroo stands about five feet tall and can weigh up to two hundred pounds. A female has the same coloring as a male, but she is somewhat smaller. A male kangaroo is called a *boomer;* a female is a *doe*.

All kangaroos are marsupials. Like other mammals, they have fur and bear live young, which they feed with milk. The unusual feature of female marsupials is that they have special pouches in which they carry their young during the early part of their lives.

A female gray kangaroo is ready to breed when she is about three years old. Then she will mate with the male that is the leader of her group. Kangaroos tend to live and move about in groups called a *mob*. Although males can mate when they are three, they usually do not get a chance until they become strong enough to challenge the leader of their mob.

Female gray kangaroo

A gray kangaroo gives birth to a single baby, called a *joey,* about five weeks after she has mated. To get ready for the birth, she finds a quiet, safe place. Then she thoroughly licks her pouch so that it will be clean for the new baby. During the birth she sits quietly until the joey is safely inside her pouch.

At the time of birth, a gray kangaroo joey is about the size of a lima bean and weighs no more than a thirtieth of an ounce (about one gram). It is pink, hairless, and does not look at all like a kangaroo. When it is born, this tiny baby is at a very early stage of development. As soon as it emerges from the birth opening, it grabs on to its mother's fur with its strong forelimbs. Then, grasping tightly, it pulls its way toward the pouch. It will finish its development here.

Although the joey cannot see, it is helped along by its sense of smell. Its mother's pouch has a certain scent that leads the baby kangaroo to it. This short journey usually takes about three minutes and is done with no help from the mother.

This tiny joey in its mother's pouch will slowly grow into a smaller version of its parent.

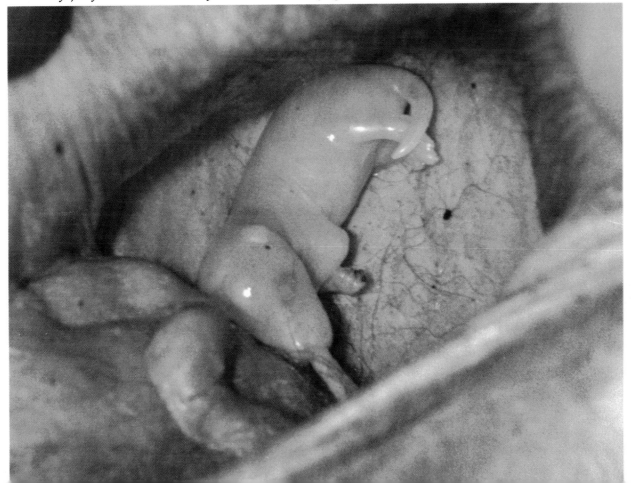

After the joey enters the pouch, it finds one of its mother's four teats. This will supply it with milk. As the joey begins to suck, the teat swells in its mouth and holds the baby tight. This keeps the joey securely fastened, so it cannot fall out of the pouch or get lost. Then, for the next five months, the joey grows into a small kangaroo inside this pouch.

At the age of about five months, the joey is ready to peek out of the pouch for the first time. Its fur is still not completely grown and its big ears flop over. Peering out cautiously with big eyes, it sniffs the fresh air and looks around. But at the slightest noise or sign of danger, it ducks back into the safety of its mother's pouch. A joey does not come all the way out of the pouch for another month or so.

When a joey is about six months old, it is finally ready to try its legs for the first time. Carefully it jumps out of the pouch. Its long, heavy tail and two big feet make a secure three-pointed base for the young kangaroo. At first it stays close to its mother, but gradually it begins to explore the world nearby. When it tires or gets hungry, it simply hops back inside the pouch and lets its mother do the walking. When entering the pouch, a joey dives in headfirst and then somersaults to turn itself around. As the joey grows, its muscles get bigger and stronger, and it can stay out of the pouch for longer periods of time.

When the Meltons' friend brought them Sport, she also brought a gunnysack lined with a sheepskin. This would be the baby kangaroo's new pouch. During the day the Meltons hung Sport's pouch outdoors. Soon he learned to hop in and out just as he had done when he lived in the wild.

By the time a joey has been in the pouch for six months, it weighs about four and a half pounds (two kilograms). Even after that, when a gray kangaroo joey is quite large, it still rides in the pouch, often peering over the top as its mother leaps across the plain. When she lies down to rest, the joey stays inside. As the joey grows, the pouch expands to make more room for it. Gray kangaroo joeys stay with their mothers longer than any other kind of kangaroo joey. After leaving the pouch, the joey stays with its mother for about ten more months, until it is nearly adult size.

A young kangaroo seems to enjoy the constant rocking movement of its mother's body. The Meltons found that one of Sport's favorite activities was going for walks. So they designed a "walking pouch" from an old knapsack, and Sport would ride in it. From his shoulder-high perch, Sport eagerly looked out as Irma walked about in the neighborhood.

As Sport grew he continued to drink milk, but he also was learning to eat grass. Young kangaroos eat both grass and milk until they become independent. In the wild they sometimes don't even bother to leave the pouch to grab a mouthful of grass!

Adult kangaroos live on a diet that includes grass, if they get a chance, and other low-growing plants. Kangaroos can eat very coarse grasses and will sometimes even eat cardboard. Their digestive systems are able to break down even these very tough fibers.

Kangaroos have sharp front teeth that are good for cutting grass, and flat molars on the sides of their mouths that are good for chewing. Unlike the jaws of most animals, the upper and lower jaws of kangaroos are not attached to each other. The teeth can slide from side to side. This way they can use their teeth like scissors to neatly slice a blade of grass in two.

Like other young animals, kangaroo joeys are playful. They poke and pull at each other and at their mothers' ears and tails. Since Sport had no other kangaroo as a playmate, he made friends with the Meltons' dog, Sheba. Sheba allowed Sport to climb on her and treated him as if he were a rather oddly shaped puppy. Sheba watched over Sport as he wandered about the yard. If he got dirty, she licked him clean.

As Sport grew, he learned to move about by hopping on his strong hind legs. Animals such as kangaroos that hop on just their hind legs are said to ricochet. Both feet leave the ground and land at the same time.

One of the most amazing features of kangaroos is their ability to leap long distances. An adult gray kangaroo can jump forty-four feet in a single bound and leap over a fence eleven feet high. Farmers and ranchers sometimes build fences to try to keep kangaroos out of their land, but they are usually not successful. The kangaroos just leap over the fences or kick holes in them to jump through.

The kangaroo uses its long, heavy tail for balance when hopping. The tail's weight keeps the kangaroo from tipping forward. When the kangaroo sits, the tail becomes a sturdy support, and with the two back feet forms a built-in three-pointed chair.

To jump, a kangaroo springs forward on its hind feet. Inside each leg is a structure called a tendon, which is like a large rubber band. When the kangaroo lands, each leg bends, and this large tendon stretches. On the next forward leap, the kangaroo's tendon contracts as if it were a rubber band snapping back to its resting shape. This pushes the kangaroo forward.

A kangaroo can hop over very long distances without tiring. It "cruises" at about eleven miles per hour but can put on bursts of speed of up to forty miles per hour. In dry seasons a kangaroo will travel up to two hundred miles searching for grass and water.

When moving about slowly, a kangaroo does not leap. Instead, it does what is called a *slow walk*. First it leans over and puts its forelimbs on the ground. Then, using the tail as a support, it swings the hind feet forward in a rocking motion and places them in front of the forelimbs. Then it moves the forelimbs forward and repeats the procedure.

The kangaroos' soft fur keeps them warm in cold or rainy weather. However, in many parts of Australia where kangaroos live, hot weather is a bigger problem than cold. When it is hot, kangaroos are more active at night and during the cooler early morning hours.

To cool off in the middle of the day, kangaroos often lie down in a shady place. Sometimes they use their feet to dig a shallow hole in which to lie. The damp earth in the hole is cool.

Kangaroos also keep cool by licking their forelimbs. Just beneath the skin of the underarm are many blood vessels. When the skin is moistened and later dries, the blood is cooled. This blood then travels to the rest of the body and cools it.

Kangaroos clean themselves by licking and scratching. Their front paws can be used almost like hands to pick off insects and to clean their fur. The fourth toe of each hind foot has two nails placed close together. These can be used like tweezers to remove ticks.

The feet of kangaroos are also powerful weapons for self-defense. To defend itself, a kangaroo leans back on its heavy tail and uses its rear feet to kick its opponent. The long, sharp nails on the center toes can make a painful gash. Kangaroos also "box" with their forelimbs.

Only male kangaroos fight among themselves. Those that are the strongest and that can fight off the others become the leaders of the mob. These strong males are the ones that mate the most often with females.

At mating time, males make a low snorting sound. The noise warns other males to keep away. Otherwise, kangaroos do not make much noise at all.

When necessary, both males and females will defend themselves, but if possible, kangaroos will run from danger rather than fight. When a female kangaroo with a joey in her pouch is being chased by an enemy such as a dingo, she may toss the joey out. This lightens her load so that she can leap faster and lead the dingo away from the joey. The joey then finds a safe place to hide. Later, when the danger has passed, the mother will return to claim her baby.

When a kangaroo joey is too big to ride in the pouch any longer but still stays with its mother, it is called a *young-at-heel*. It may wander away for short periods but usually stays close to its mother's side to feed and rest. During this time the mother is getting ready to mate again. By the time her new joey is born, the young-at-heel is able to be on its own and live entirely on grass. Even so, the young-at-heel may continue to drink milk from one of the remaining three teats until it is no longer allowed to do so. After leaving its mother, the young kangaroo will stay in the same mob, at least for a while.

When Sport was a little more than a year old, he was ready to be on his own. He no longer needed milk and was able to eat grass well. The Meltons did not have to take care of him any longer.

Sport had become tame during his stay with the Meltons. Unlike wild kangaroos, he was not afraid of people. His new home would have to be a nature preserve, where he would be safe from hunters. Because he was so friendly, Sport would live in a special enclosure, where people could come close and pet him.

Sport made many friends while he was with the Meltons. Les Melton's mother was particularly fond of Sport and often helped care for him.

The Meltons were sad to have to part with Sport, but they knew it was best for him to live outdoors with other kangaroos. There he would be with his own kind and would have plenty of room to run and jump. It would almost be like living in the wild.

Some kangaroos live to be twenty years old, but for most the normal life span is seven years.

Kangaroos have lived in Australia for a very long time. Scientists believe marsupials first came to Australia about 49 million years ago. They came from South America through Antarctica at a time when all the continents were much closer together. Today, of the 250 types of marsupials in the world, 170 of them live in Australia or on neighboring islands. Except for the opossum, which lives in the United States and Canada, the rest live in Central America.

The kangaroo has long been a symbol of Australia. It appears on the national coat of arms, and on coins, stamps, and airplanes as well.

Today, as farming and industry alter the Australian landscape, the survival of some kinds of kangaroos and other marsupials is endangered. Often people do not realize how they affect the lives of other creatures when they change the environment. Only as we learn more about these fascinating animals can we better know how kangaroos and people can best live together in the future.

INDEX

Photographs are in **boldface**

aborigines, 10
Australia, 5, 6, 9, 13, 44, 46
   explorers in, 10
   kangaroo as symbol for, 44

bettong, rufous, **13**
boomer (*see* kangaroo, gray, male)

dingoes (*see* dogs, wild)
doe (*see* kangaroo, gray, female)
dogs, wild, 9

farmers, 10, 33

kangaroo, gray, 14
   birth of, 15, 16, 17
   cleaning habits, 36, **36**
   diet, 29
   feet, 13, 21, 36, **36**, 37, **37**
   female, 14, **15**, 16, **16**, **17**, **20**, 21, 24, 38
   fighting, 37, **37**, 38
   hopping, 31, **32**, 33
   hunting of, 9, 10
   joey, 16
      in the pouch, 16, 17, **17**, 18, **19**, 20, 21, 24, **24**, 25
      leaving pouch for first time, 21
   keeping warm and cool, 35, **35**
   life span, 44
   male, 14, **14**, 37, **37**, 38, **38**
   mating, 15, 37, 38
   mobs, 15
   slow walking, 34, **34**
   tail, 21, 33, 34
   teeth, 29
   young-at-heel, 40, **41**
kangaroo, red, **12**, 13

macropods, 13
marsupials, 14–15, 44, 46
Melton, Irma and Les, 5
   care of Sport, 5, 6, **6**, 7, 22
   permit to keep Sport, 6, 7
   walking with Sport, **3**, 26, **26–27**
Mrs. Melton (Les's mother), 43, **42**

opossums, 44

potoroids, 13

ranchers, 10, 33

Sheba (the Meltons' dog), 31, **31**
Sport, **4**, 7, 14, **42**
   care of, 6
   diet, 6, **6**, **28**, 29
   hopping, **30**, 31
   in his pouch, 22, **22**, **23**, 26, **27**
   in nature preserve, 43
   rescue of, 5

wallaby, agile, **13**